HOW IT'S MADE
TORAH SCROLL

by Allison Ofanansky • Photographs by Eliyahu Alpern

APPLES & HONEY PRESS

Milburn, NJ • Jerusalem

We would like to thank the many people who shared their time and knowledge with us:

Gabriel Bass, Bass Synagogue Furniture, Moshav Mata, Israel, http://basssynagoguefurniture.com/
Zacchariah ben-Moshe and Neot Kedumim, The Biblical Landscape Reserve in Israel, www.neot-kedumim.org.il
Yosef Efrati, Tzfat Israel
Shoshana Gugenheim, Women of the Book, Moshav Aviezer, Israel, www.womenofthebook.org
Ja'el Batyah Hatch, Studio Tiferet Hayetsirah, Yavniel, Israel, http://jaelbatyah.wix.com/studiotiferet
Shmuel Hershkovitz, Hershkovitz Atzei Chaim for Torah Scrolls, Bnei Brak, Israel
Simcha Katsof, Hilltop Scribe, Safsufa, Israel www.hilltopscribe.com
Hannah Klebansky, Jerusalem, Israel
Romy Krassenstein, Kodesh Judaica and Holy Seeds, Sydney, Australia
Rabbi Linda Motzkin, Bread and Torah, Saratoga Springs, New York, http://breadandtorah.org/
Sheva Chaya Servetter, Sheva Chaya Gallery, Tzfat, Israel, http://www.shevachaya.com/
Yossi Shoa and Shuki Freiman, Shuki Freiman Handmade Artwork, Jerusalem, Israel, http://www.sfreiman.com/
Gadi Turner, Otzer HaSTaM of Tzfat, Israel, www.hastam.com
Yitzchok Weiss, Klaf Roseman, Bnei Brak, Israel, http://www.klafroseman.co.il/

The publisher wishes to credit the following sources of additional photographs:
Shutterstock: back cover yad: blueeyes, 13 girl: Asier Romero, 15 feather: Jakub Krechowicz, 15 scissors: MNI, 21 pen: Galushko Sergey, 21 berries:
Elena Schweitzer, 25 case: kavram, 26 text: blueeyes, 27 clay: tescha555, 32 craft: Green Leaf. Gili Shani, www.gilishani.com: 3 hide, 12 man, 18-19
parchment making and tool. University of Bologna: 8 scroll. Andrew Tertes: 9 woman. Linda Motzkin: 17 teens. Jonathan Rubenstein: 1, 19 stretching.
Hannah Klebansky: 23 papercut. Ruby Feilich: 24 beadwork. David Hollander, Hollander Photographic Services, www.hollanderphoto.net: 31 top.
Tom Verniero: 31 bottom. www.jewishpeople.com: 32 outline. Yossi Shoa and Shuki Frieman shukifreimanstudio@gmail.com: 32 Torah.

Apples & Honey Press
An imprint of Behrman House and Gefen Publishing House
Behrman House, 11 Edison Place, Springfield, New Jersey 07081
Gefen Publishing House Ltd., 6 Hatzvi Street, Jerusalem 94386, Israel
www.applesandhoneypress.com

Library of Congress Cataloging-in-Publication Data

Names: Ofanansky, Allison, author. | Alpern, Eliyahu, photographer.
Title: How it's made : Torah scroll / by Allison Ofanansky ;
photographs by Eliyahu Alpern.
Description: Springfield, NJ : Apples & Honey Press, [2016]
Identifiers: LCCN 2015043360 | ISBN 9781681155166
Subjects: LCSH: Torah scrolls—Juvenile literature.
Classification: LCC BM659.S3 O33 2016 | DDC 296.4/615—dc23 LC
record available at http://lccn.loc.gov/2015043360 http://lccn.loc.
gov/2015043360

Design by Elynn Cohen
Edited by Dena Neusner
Printed in United States
9 8 7 6 5 4 3 2

For thousands of years, the Jewish people have been making Torah scrolls like this one.

Many people put hard work, skill, knowledge, and love into making each and every Torah scroll.

Have you ever wondered how a Torah scroll is made?

Stretching hide for parchment

Making ink

Writing a Torah scroll

Weaving cloth for a Torah cover

Making a glass yad

Let's find out . . .

3

But first . . . what is the Torah?

The Torah is the holiest text of the Jewish people. The Hebrew word Torah תורה means "teaching."

The Torah tells the biblical stories of the creation of the world and the birth of the Jewish people. It provides commandments and teachings about how we should live.

What does the word "Torah" mean to YOU?

The Jewish people have handed the Torah down from generation to generation by carefully copying its words into special scrolls and reading from those scrolls.

4

What is a Torah scroll?

Do you know the difference between a Torah scroll and a Hebrew Bible? Match each description to the correct picture

- Handwritten
- Printed
- Paper
- Parchment
- Bound as a book
- Scroll rolled onto poles
- Kept in a special cabinet
- Kept on a bookshelf

- Read at special times
- May be read at any time
- Written in Hebrew
- May be written in any language
- Includes only the Five Books of Moses
- Includes much more than the Five Books of Moses

32

Number of times the word "Torah" appears in a Torah scroll

"People involved in every stage of making a Torah must have the proper intention. They must always think: This is for a holy Torah."

—Zacchariah ben-Moshe, *sofer* (scribe)

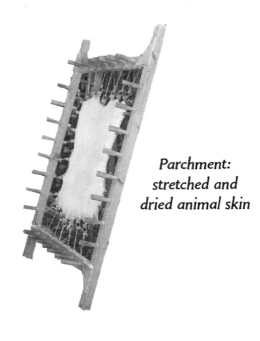

Parchment: stretched and dried animal skin

Ink

Feather or reed pens

What do we need to make a Torah scroll?

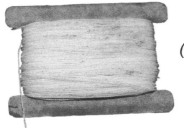

Sinew (special thread)

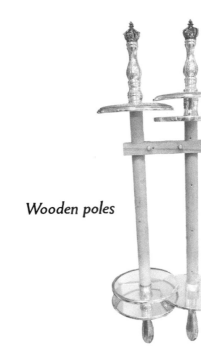

Concentration and devotion

Decorations

Cover

Wooden poles

7

Tradition and change

In many ways, Torah scrolls today are made just as they have been made for thousands of years. Not a single letter has been changed. Many of the same materials are used now as in ancient times. Much of the work is still done by hand. But some things are done differently.

Modern materials and machines are used for some tasks, such as molding silver decorations.

800 years
Age of the oldest complete Torah scroll

All Torah scrolls written today have 42 lines in each column, but this ancient scroll from Italy has 45 lines in each column.

Shoshana Gugenheim decided to write a Torah scroll because of her "passion for the Torah and all things handmade."

Another change is that traditionally Torah scribes have all been men, but today some women write Torah scrolls.

What traditions do YOU like to keep?

What traditions would you like to change?

Who writes Torah scrolls?

A person who writes Torah scrolls and other holy Jewish texts is called a *sofer*. To become a *sofer* a person learns how to write the Hebrew script used in Torah scrolls, as well as all the rules for writing a kosher Torah.

Would **YOU** like to write a Torah scroll?

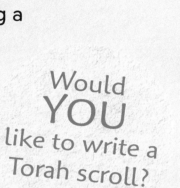

Simcha Katsof *reads every word out loud before writing it. "Saying the words gives them breath and life," he says.*

Hannah Klebansky *learned to be a sofer when she moved to Israel from the former Soviet Union. "Every Jewish person should write a Torah scroll," she says. "It changes your life."*

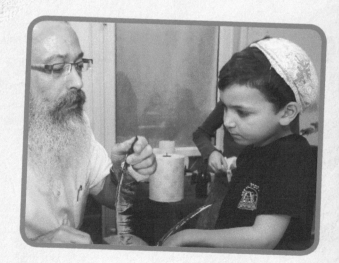

Gadi Turner *works at an educational center in Israel, where he teaches people of all ages about Torah scrolls. "This type of writing is not only beautiful artwork, it's also spiritual. Writing a Torah scroll connects the sofer to God," he says.*

וַיֹּאמֶר הַשָּׁאֵת תְּלַקְרוֹלְבוּ אֶת לְקָרֹלְבַכֶם

Sofer styles

Look at these passages from different Torah scrolls. They are written in fancy scripts. Some of the letters have crowns on top. Some letters are wider than others.

This is a "recycled" Torah scroll. It contains pieces from several scrolls that had been damaged. Can you see that the style of the letters is not exactly the same in these two columns?

Take a closer look

Writing letters in a Torah scroll

"Each sofer has a different style, because the person's soul is in the letters."

—Simcha Katsof, *sofer*

No crooked lines allowed!

Before a *sofer* starts to write, lines and columns are marked on the parchment.

The lines are hard to see, because they are etched by hand with a metal tool, not drawn with ink.

42
Number of lines in each column of Torah text

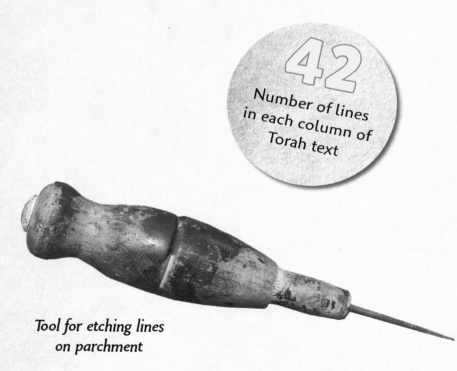

Tool for etching lines on parchment

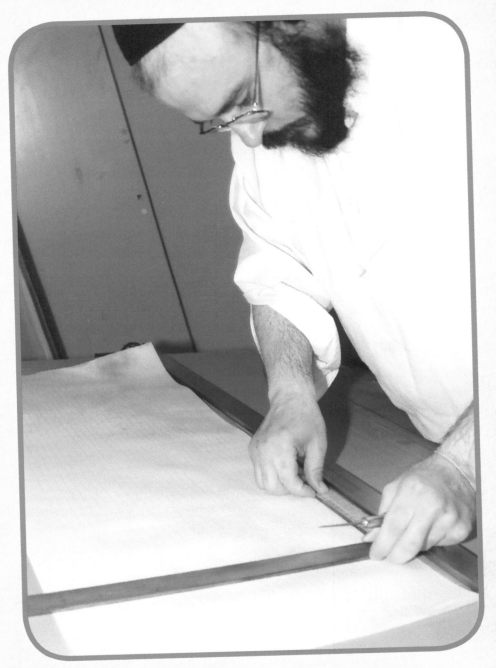

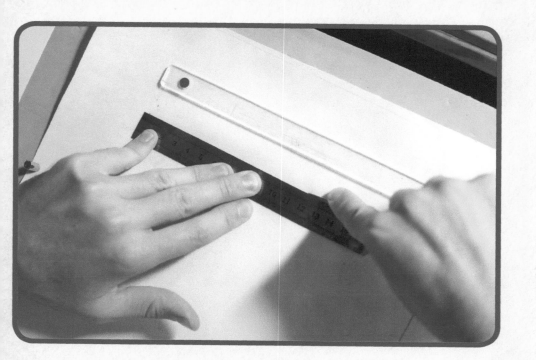

Write on a blank unlined page

Try to write perfectly straight on a blank page. It's not easy!

Take a closer look

Writing on pre-etched lines

Today, computers help measure the lines, but they are still etched by hand.

Is your writing straight or crooked?

13

Sofer Simcha Katsof makes a quill pen from a feather.

He chooses a feather . . .

trims it to the right length . . .

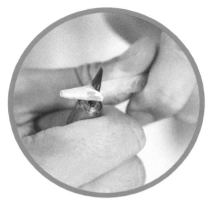

cuts off the tip . . .

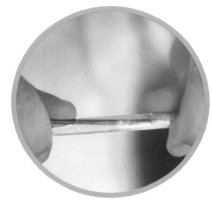

hollows out a channel for the ink . . .

. . . and shapes the tip using a sharp knife.

Before using a new quill to write on the Torah scroll parchment, he tests it on a scrap of paper.

A sofer's pen

Can a Torah be written with a ballpoint pen? A pencil? A crayon? No! It must be written with a feather quill or reed pen dipped in ink. A *sofer* goes through many quills writing a whole Torah scroll.

14

Write with a feather quill pen

With scissors, carefully cut off the tip of a feather, at an angle. Hollow out the end with a toothpick. You now have a quill pen!

Dip your quill in ink. (Use the recipe for ink on page 21, or use washable paint.) Write your name on a piece of paper with the quill and ink. Can you also write your Hebrew name?

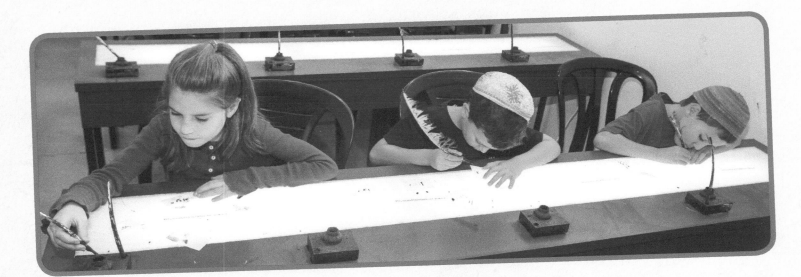

The sofer copies directly from a book or a photocopy.

Oops! What if the sofer makes a mistake?

In a Torah scroll, there can't be any mistakes. Not a single letter can be missing. Each one must be perfect. They cannot touch, or be blurry, or be incomplete.

To prevent mistakes, a *sofer* cannot write from memory.

Rabbi Yosef Efrati checks every word and every letter for mistakes.

The sofer may use a light table to trace the letters.

304,805
The number of letters in a Torah scroll

The sofer can use a computer program that scans the text and checks for mistakes.

"The Torah is our instruction manual for life. It cannot have any mistakes."

—Yosef Efrati, *sofer*

The *sofer* fixes mistakes very carefully.

The sofer scrapes the ink off the parchment using a razor blade . . .

smooths the parchment with sandpaper . . .

. . . and carefully rewrites the word.

How do **YOU** fix mistakes?

Teens proofreading panels of Torah as part of a community Torah-making project

Why do YOU think we take such care to make Torah scrolls?

Parchment-maker Yitzchok Weiss soaks the skins in a tub of limewater for several days to soften them and get the hair off.

Yemenite-style parchment made from deer skin and dyed with herbs

What is a Torah scroll made of?

The parchment, the ink, and even the wooden rollers that hold a Torah scroll are all carefully made according to tradition.

What is parchment, anyway?

A Torah scroll is written on parchment, which is made from animal skins. The skins must be from kosher animals—usually cows, but also sheep, goats, or deer.

A machine scrapes the skins clean. In the past, workers scraped them clean with knives—a difficult and dirty job!

Rabbi Linda Motzkin teaches community members how to stretch a deer skin, to make parchment for a Torah scroll.

Parchment-maker Shmuel Weiss stretches skins on a frame.

This machine smooths the parchment so it has no rough spots or holes.

Take a closer look

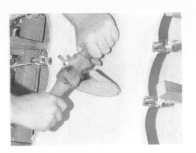

Tool used to scrape drying parchment

19

A recipe for Torah ink

The recipe for making ink for a Torah scroll is thousands of years old. *Sofer* Zacchariah ben-Moshe shows us how it's done.

Ingredients for making ink

Directions

FIRST say, "I am making this ink to write a Torah scroll." This step cannot be left out. Grind gallnuts into a powder. Grind dried tree sap into a powder. Mix together gallnut and tree sap powders. Add dried, ground pomegranate peels. Add enough water to make a thin soup. Add a pinch of copper acetate. Stir—the white liquid will quickly turn black! Cook over low heat for five hours until the ink thickens.

Grinding ingredients with mortar and pestle

The magic ingredient: copper acetate. This mineral has a chemical reaction with the acid in the gallnuts, which turns the ink black.

Mixing the ingredients together in a cup of water

Tree sap makes ink shiny and helps it stick to the parchment. Sap from the acacia tree (called gum arabic) is often used in making ink. It is also an ingredient in many candies!

Gallnuts are not really nuts. They are growths caused by wasps laying their eggs on a tree. Gallnuts give the ink a strong and long-lasting color.

Make your own ink

This ink can't be used for writing Torah scrolls—but it's fun to make!

Ingredients

- 1 cup fresh berries
- 1 teaspoon white vinegar
- 1 teaspoon salt

Directions

1. Crush the berries.
2. Push them through a strainer over a bowl to collect the juice.
3. Mix the vinegar and salt with the juice.
4. Write with this ink using your quill pen.

Putting it all together

Using a needle and special thread (made from animal sinew), the craftsman sews the finished pieces of parchment together.

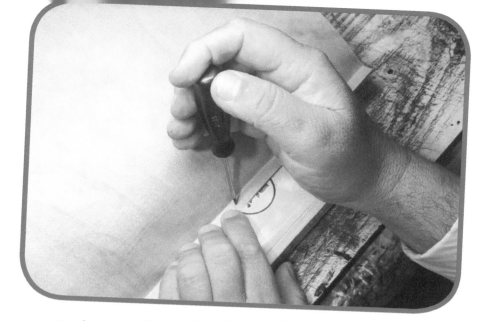

He lays two pieces of parchment with the blank sides out and makes a small fold in along the edges . . .

pokes holes in the parchment . . .

. . . and sews them together with the needle and sinew.

Display of rollers for Torah scrolls

Tree of Life

The Torah scroll is held by two sturdy rollers, which may be decorated, painted, engraved, or covered with silver. This roller is called an *eitz chayim*, which means "tree of life" in Hebrew.

Handle with silver decorations and engraved names

Take a closer look

Carving the wood handle

Painted and decorated handle

"It is a tree of life to those who hold on to it."
—from Proverbs 3:18, about the Torah

How does a Torah scroll get dressed up?

When a Torah scroll isn't being read, it is rolled up and held together with a belt.

There are no pictures or drawings on a Torah scroll—only words. But the scroll is dressed in a beautiful cover that can be decorated in many styles and colors.

"*The clothing for a Torah is like the royal robe worn by a king.*"
—Romy Krassenstein, artist

Take a closer look

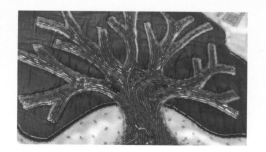

Beadwork on a Torah cover

Artist Ja'el Batyah Hatch weaves a Torah cover.

She starts with sheep wool . . .

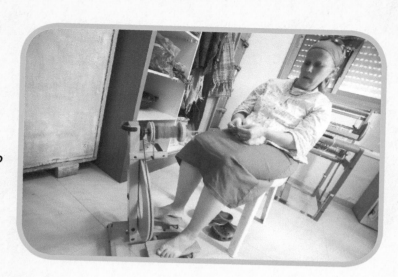

spins it into thread . . .

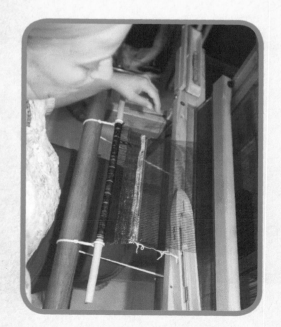

". . . and weaves the thread into cloth."

"The Torah cover is like the Jewish people: Each of us is a thread in the tapestry, a part of the pattern."

—Ja'el Batyah Hatch, artist

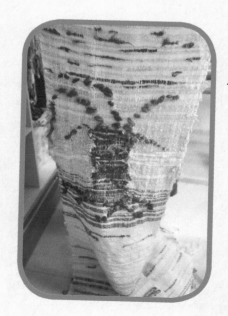

She sews the finished cloth into a Torah cover.

Silver or wooden cases for Torah scrolls are popular among Jewish communities from the Middle East.

Like royalty

The Torah scroll, dressed in its woven cover, is topped with a beautifully crafted crown and other decorations.

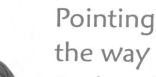

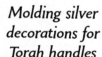

Silver crown

Molding silver decorations for Torah handles

Pointing the way

Torah readers use a pointer called a *yad* (which means "hand" in Hebrew). This way the reader doesn't touch the parchment and get it dirty or smudge the letters.

Sheva Chaya Servetter makes a glass *yad*.

She heats a glass rod to make it soft and flexible . . .

Antique silver breastplate

"Decorating the Torah scroll reminds us that this is not just a regular book. The decorations help us remember that it is holy."
–Shmuel Hershkovitz, *eitz chayim* manufacturer

shapes the hand and pointer finger in the gas flame . . .

. . . and adds a design with glass
of a different color.

The finished glass yad

Make a *yad*

Using clay, roll it into a long
handle. Shape a small
hand on the
end with
a pointing
finger.
When it
dries, you
can paint it.

"*The Torah is a shining light that
guides us through life.*"

—Sheva Chaya Servetter, *artist*

27

A home for a Torah scroll

A Torah scroll is kept in a special cabinet called a Holy Ark, or *Aron Kodesh*.

An Aron Kodesh with designs based on biblical stories

Gabriel Bass smooths the wood for an Ark.

"*An Aron Kodesh, like all ceremonial art, tells a story. I like to use images from the Torah.*"

—Gabriel Bass, artist

28

Celebrate!

The ink is dry. The *sofer* has finished writing every letter without a mistake. The long scroll of parchment is wound onto the rollers. The Torah is decorated and ready to be taken to the synagogue.

Mazel tov!

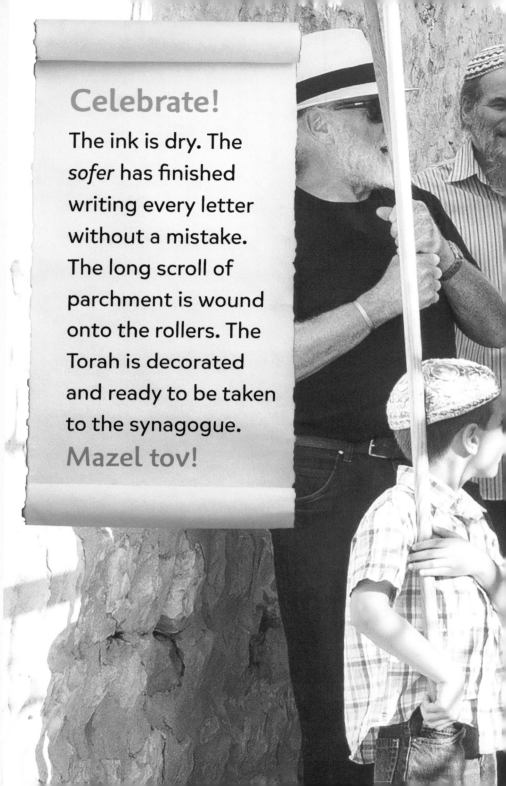

How do YOU celebrate when you finish a big project?

How do we read from the Torah?

All of this hard work and preparation leads up to this moment . . . when we read from the Torah! It takes a lot of practice to read from the Torah. The words are in Hebrew, and there are no vowels!

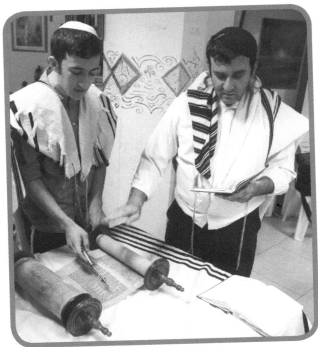

People come up to the Torah to say the blessing before each section is read.

0

The number of periods, commas, question marks, and exclamation points in a Torah scroll

Torah scrolls come in many sizes. Small Torahs are easy to carry—wherever you go!

Many people read from the Torah for the first time at their bar or bat mitzvah.

How do
YOU
think it would
feel to read
from a Torah
scroll?

Design a Torah scroll cover

Draw your design for a Torah cover. What kinds of materials will you use for decoration?

2 inches

The size of the smallest known Torah scroll

www.ingramcontent.com/pod-product-compliance
Lightning Source LLC
Jackson TN
JSHW041632161224

75386JS00065B/421